ALTERNATOR
BOOKS™

MYSTERIES OF THE
GREAT WALL
OF CHINA

Karen Latchana Kenney

Lerner Publications ◆ Minneapolis

To the history detectives of the world, whose discoveries help us understand our past

Lerner Publications Company
A division of Lerner Publishing Group, Inc.
241 First Avenue North
Minneapolis, MN 55401 USA

For reading levels and more information, look up this title at www.lernerbooks.com.

Main body text set in Aptifer Slab LT Pro Regular 11.5/18.
Typeface provided by Linotype AG.

Library of Congress Cataloging-in-Publication Data

Names: Kenney, Karen Latchana, author.
Title: Mysteries of the Great Wall of China / by Karen Latchana
   Kenney.
Description: Minneapolis : Lerner Publications, 2018. | Series: Ancient
   mysteries | Includes bibliographical references and index.
Identifiers: LCCN 2016048100 (print) | LCCN 2016050338 (ebook) | ISBN
   9781512440133 (lb : alk. paper) | ISBN 9781512449228 (eb pdf)
Subjects: LCSH: Great Wall of China (China)—Juvenile literature.
Classification: LCC DS793.G67 K46 2018 (print) | LCC DS793.G67 (ebook)
   | DDC 931—dc23

LC record available at https://lccn.loc.gov/2016048100

Manufactured in the United States of America
1-42275-26132-3/6/2017

TABLE OF CONTENTS

INTRODUCTION
A LONG FORGOTTEN WALL

An ancient atlas held a clue that British researcher William Lindesay couldn't resist. It showed a section of a wall in the Gobi Desert region of southern Mongolia. Locally, it was known as the Wall of Genghis, after the once-powerful Mongolian leader Genghis Khan.

Lindesay had been curious about the wall since 1997, when a friend gave him the atlas that had been written in the twelfth century. Lindesay had a suspicion that the wall wasn't actually Mongolian at all.

Lindesay contacted an expert on Mongolian geography, Professor Baasan Tudevin, who had traveled throughout the Gobi Desert. He had seen different structures there and suggested using Google Earth to locate the wall. Amazingly, in the Google Earth images, Tudevin and Lindesay saw a thin black line where the atlas showed the wall.

DIGGING FOR CHINA

Lindesay wondered if this could be a section of China's Great Wall. He knew that sections of the wall came close to the border between Mongolia and China and that this border had not always been clearly defined. He also knew that the wall's beginning and end are unknown. Many of its sections are crumbling and **deteriorated**, so they hardly look like walls at all.

In August 2011, Lindesay led an expedition into the desert to find the wall and determine if it was Chinese or not. On the second day, the team found the wall. It was shoulder-high in some places and ran for 62 miles

William Lindesay

(100 kilometers) through the desert and up an extinct volcano. And much of the wall looked just like part of the Great Wall that stands in Gansu, China.

How have parts of the wall survived for thousands of years? What was the wall made of? And where does the wall begin and end? People have many questions about this incredible relic of the past. And the Great Wall of China still has secrets to reveal.

CHAPTER 1

AN ANCIENT SYSTEM

From Old Dragon's Head—a section of the Great Wall that stretches into the Bohai Sea—the Great Wall of China climbs mountains, crosses valleys and plains, and zigzags into the country's western desert. Its earliest remnants were constructed more than two thousand years ago.

Some parts of the wall are made of brick and stone. Other parts are crumbling earthen and stick masses that have worn down over time. Together, they mark the edge of China's northern frontier.

The most famous part of the wall is known as Badaling. This section reaches as high as 25 feet (7.5 meters) and is 20 feet (6 m) wide. From Badaling the wall stretches for miles. Yet this is only one section of an entire system of walls including watchtowers and forts. The system also includes natural barriers such as hills and rivers. The sections of the wall are not all connected, and they cover vast areas of land.

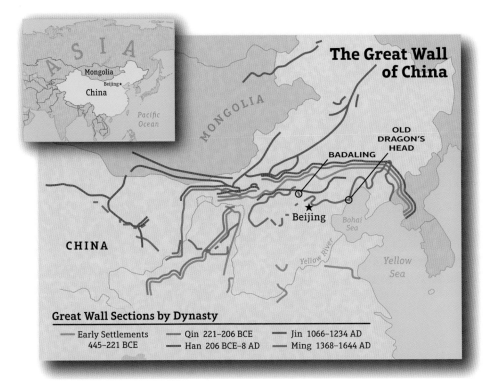

The Great Wall of China

OLD DRAGON'S HEAD

BADALING

MONGOLIA

Beijing

Bohai Sea

CHINA

Yellow River

Yellow Sea

ASIA

Mongolia
Beijing
China

Pacific Ocean

Great Wall Sections by Dynasty

— Early Settlements 445–221 BCE
— Qin 221–206 BCE
— Han 206 BCE–8 AD
— Jin 1066–1234 AD
— Ming 1368–1644 AD

ONGOING MYSTERY

Over the centuries, people have tried to figure out exactly how long the Great Wall of China is. Some thought it was only 1,200 miles (1,931 km) long. Others believed it was more than 30,000 miles (48,000 km) long. Because parts of the wall are in remote areas

An image of Mongolia and China taken from space

MYTH ALERT!

One of the best-known myths about the Great Wall is that it is visible from the moon. This myth, which started in the late nineteenth century, stated that the wall would be the only human-made object seen from the moon. The wall is actually impossible to see with the human eye from space, but it can be seen from that distance using radar-imaging techniques.

and many parts have been destroyed, researchers aren't sure how long the Great Wall was, and only the four longest sections of the wall have been well documented. They were built during the Qin, Han, Jin, and Ming Dynasties, long periods of rule in China. An official Chinese study in early 2012 stated that the wall's total length was 13,170 miles (21,196 km). Yet this number may never be final, as new sections of the wall continue to be discovered, while other sections decay.

A section of the Great Wall near Beijing is a popular destination for tourists, but it is falling into disrepair.

CHAPTER 2
CLASHING CULTURES

Before the wall was built, China was protected on three sides by the Himalayas at the south, the Pacific Ocean at the east, and the Tibetan Plateau at the west. But the north was open and unprotected. The northern frontier was where two very different cultures collided: the Chinese and the Mongolians.

Chinese culture had developed over thousands of years. Farming began in the north in about 8000 BCE. Many farmers lived in permanent dwellings in different settlements. **Nomadic** Mongolian peoples lived nearby. They lived in tents and raised livestock, moving from pasture to pasture. Their land was not suitable for farming, so the nomads relied on trade with Chinese farmers to get the goods they could not make, such as grain and metal.

A painting from the Northern Song Dynasty (960-1127) shows Chinese farmers at work.

The Chinese considered the nomadic peoples to be **barbarians**. The Chinese eventually refused to trade with the Mongolians, and the Mongolians attacked Chinese settlements to take the goods they needed. The first record of a major attack is found in a poem from the ninth century BCE.

A SYSTEM FOR DEFENSE

Most researchers believe that walls became the main Chinese defense system against attacks from Mongolians. The earliest walls were built by the individual settlements. These settlements were unified

This twentieth-century illustration depicts Chinese soldiers from around 1000 BCE.

A Chinese drawing shows Emperor Qin mapping the Great Wall.

under **Emperor** Qin during the Qin Dynasty (221–206 BCE). Emperor Qin had the early walls removed. Then construction of a single, long wall began. Historian Sima Qian recorded its construction in 214 BCE, writing that the wall stretched for 10,000 *li*. A li is a traditional Chinese measurement—slightly less than 1 mile, or 1.6 km, is equal to about 3 li.

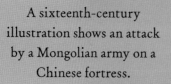

SOLDIERS ON GUARD

Old military manuals tell us what happened when there was a threat of attack. Chinese soldiers stationed at towers along the Great Wall went into action. They set fires at night, made smoke signals during the day, waved flags, and fired cannons. Wolf dung was thought to make the tallest, straightest plumes of smoke. These different signals indicated how big the threat was and how many soldiers were needed. For example, five cannon shots and fires meant ten thousand soldiers should be sent.

Signals were passed from tower to tower until the message reached military command. Then troops could be sent to the site of the threat. Messages like this could travel 620 miles (1,000 km) along the wall in a day. That's much faster than a person could ride on horseback. With this system, military commanders at the wall could send messages all the way to the emperor in Beijing.

CHAPTER 3
BUILDING THE DRAGON

A Chinese folk name perfectly describes the first northern walls—earth dragon. Built from compacted soil, reeds, twigs, and rocks, these earthen walls snaked across the Chinese landscape.

After the rule of Emperor Qin, other Chinese emperors rebuilt and expanded the northern walls. They mostly used building materials that came from the places where the walls were located.

BUILT TO LAST

The best-preserved sections of the Great Wall were built over two hundred years during the Ming Dynasty. These are the most recognizable stone and brick sections of the Great Wall. These sections, which span 5,499 miles (8,851 km), were built from **quarried** stone and oven-fired bricks. Some had to be transported great distances to be used on the wall.

A brick section of the Great Wall near Beijing

MYTH ALERT!

Was rice used to build the wall? It sounds crazy, but it's true! Scientists tested **mortar** used between bricks on the wall. They found it contained a **carbohydrate** that's in sticky rice. This showed that ancient Chinese builders added sticky rice soup to **calcium carbonate**. This made a superstrong mortar that's helped keep parts of the wall together for centuries.

A BACKBREAKING TASK

The backbreaking work of hauling and building was done by forced laborers, including soldiers, farmers, and criminals. It was common practice in ancient China to use forced laborers for public construction projects. Throughout the country's history, the wall was often the biggest construction project.

The Ming Great Wall must have been especially difficult to work on because of its size and the materials it was made of. People have long wondered how it was built. Some believe workers and animals carried heavy bricks along flat ground. Where it was

An artist's illustration shows laborers building the wall while Chinese soldiers defend the outside.

A twentieth-century illustration shows laborers building the Great Wall while soldiers and Chinese rulers watch.

more difficult to travel, they passed bricks and stone up mountainsides from person to person. And if that was impossible, workers chiseled walls straight out of the mountains. For their hard work, laborers suffered. The work was exhausting, they weren't given enough food or clothing, and they were often mistreated by those in charge.

Historians estimate that close to one million laborers died during the wall's construction. Some people believe that the workers were buried inside the wall. Could it be the world's longest cemetery? Archaeologists have found peoples' remains near the wall, but none have yet been found inside the wall.

A painting of slaves building the Great Wall

CHAPTER 4
A CRUMBLING TREASURE

The Great Wall's major construction ended in 1644, at the fall of the Ming Dynasty. The wall couldn't stop invaders from conquering Beijing in 1644. The Ming emperor had asked for help from the Manchus, people from nearby Manchuria. Instead, the Manchus took power and ruled China for the next 250 years.

They worked with their northern neighbors. Invasion became less of a problem, and the wall became less important as a defensive structure. It fell into ruin and disrepair and became a reminder of the lives lost in building it and China's military failure.

RESTORING A RELIC

But the wall rose again as a symbol of Chinese engineering and skill. Missionaries in the seventeenth century wrote about China's achievements in building the wall. European traders and explorers admired the incredible structure, and legends of it spread. The wall eventually became a tourist site. The government has restored parts of it, especially the most famous section of the Ming Great Wall at Badaling. Thousands of tourists visit this site every day. And the United Nations Educational, Scientific and Cultural Organization (UNESCO) declared the Great Wall a World Heritage site in 1987.

Tourists explore the Great Wall near Badaling.

A crumbling section of the Great Wall

Certain sections of the wall are maintained, but much of it is vanishing. After decades of war in the country, by the early 1950s, the wall had been badly damaged. Peasants used the bricks to build homes and added soil from the wall's inner core to their fields. Roads have been built through parts of the wall. And sand and water are eroding it. China created laws in 2006 to protect the wall, but they are difficult to enforce in remote areas. In 2015 China's State Administration of Cultural Heritage estimated that 30 percent of the wall was gone and another 736 miles (1,185 km) were in poor condition. In late 2016, the Chinese government used concrete, sand, and other materials to pave over 5 miles (8 km) of the wall. The bad repair caused outrage around the world. People were horrified that China was not properly preserving one of the world's most ancient structures.

A Chinese worker repairs a section of the Great Wall in Beijing.

How much longer will the legendary Great Wall of China last? And what more can be discovered about it? We may never understand everything about this ancient relic. But in 2015, nine new sections of the wall were found in northwest China. What will further research reveal?

SCIENCE SPOTLIGHT
3-D MAPS

To find parts of the Great Wall that need to be repaired, the Chinese government is making 3-D maps of its many sections. To do this, China is using helicopter drones to take aerial images. The drones are remote-controlled flying cameras. An operator can pick specific locations for the drones to map. The drones' cameras scan small sections of the wall at a time and can precisely measure the height of the wall and its towers. The cameras also gather information about the land and plants around the wall.

A 2016 photo taken from a drone shows a section of the Great Wall near Beijing.

TIMELINE

221–206 BCE | The Qin Dynasty unites China and builds the first northern border wall.

214 BCE | Historian Sima Qian records that the Qin wall spans 10,000 li, or about 3,100 miles (5,000 km).

1368–1644 CE | The Ming Dynasty rules China. It builds the strongest and newest sections of the Great Wall.

1644 | Invaders from Manchuria overthrow the Ming Dynasty, and the Great Wall falls into disrepair.

1987 | UNESCO declares the Great Wall a World Heritage site.

2006 | China enacts laws to protect the Great Wall from human damage.

2011 | William Lindesay's expedition finds 62 miles (100 km) of the Great Wall in the Gobi Desert.

2012 | A Chinese study announces the total length of the Great Wall is 13,170 miles (21,196 km).

2015 | China's State Administration of Cultural Heritage estimates that 30 percent of the wall is gone and another 736 miles (1,185 km) of the wall is in poor condition. Nine new sections of the Great Wall are discovered in northwestern China.

GLOSSARY

barbarians: uncivilized people

calcium carbonate: a substance found in rocks, especially limestone

carbohydrate: a substance that is made of carbon, hydrogen, and oxygen and that is found in foods such as rice and bread

deteriorated: fallen apart over time

emperor: a male ruler of an empire

mortar: a building material spread between bricks or stones to hold them together

nomadic: relating to groups of people who do not live in permanent dwellings and who move from place to place for hunting or herding

quarried: taken from a quarry, a source of stone or other materials

radiocarbon: a decaying form of carbon, an element found in all living and once-living things

FURTHER INFORMATION

Coupe, Robert. *The Great Wall of China*. New York: PowerKids, 2013.

Demuth, Patricia Brennan. *Where Is the Great Wall?* New York: Grosset & Dunlap, 2015.

Great Wall Facts
http://www.chinahighlights.com/greatwall/fact

Mooney, Carla. *Great Wall of China*. Vero Beach, FL: Rourke Educational Media, 2015.

New Seven Wonders of the World: Great Wall of China
https://world.new7wonders.com/wonders/great-wall-of-china-220-b-c -and-1368-1644-a-d-china

Ransom, Candice. *Tools and Treasures of Ancient China*. Minneapolis: Lerner Publications, 2014.

TimeMaps: Ancient China
http://www.timemaps.com/civilization-ancient-china

UNESCO: The Great Wall
http://whc.unesco.org/en/list/438

INDEX

PHOTO ACKNOWLEDGMENTS

The images in this book are used with the permission of: Gordan/Shutterstock.com, p. 1 (grunge frame throughout); © iStockphoto.com/sdlgzps, p. 1; © Lost Horizon Images/Getty Images, p. 4; © Du Bin/The New York Times/Redux, p. 6; © Martin Puddy/Getty Images, p. 8; © Laura Westlund/Independent Picture Service, p. 9; NASA, p. 10; Moonbrush/Alamy Stock Photo, p. 11; Ivan Kmit/Alamy Stock Photo, p. 12; © NW China/Bridgeman Images, p. 13; © The Stapleton Collection/Bridgeman Images, p. 14; The Granger Collection, New York, p. 15; © HIP/Art Resource, NY, p. 16; TAO Images Limited/Alamy Stock Photo, p. 18; © OTHK/Getty Images, p. 19; PlanetNextDoor/Alamy Stock Photo, p. 20; © Look and Learn/Bridgeman Images, pp. 21, 22; © HSIEN-MIN YANG/National Geographic Creative, p. 23; Glow Asia RF/Alamy Stock Photo, p. 24; imageBROKER/Alamy Stock Photo, p. 25; © Sino Images/Getty Images, p. 26; © TEH ENG KOON/AFP/Getty Images, p. 27; Xinhua/Alamy Stock Photo, p. 28.

Front cover: © iStockphoto.com/sdlgzps.